ROYAL
MEMORABILIA

Text ©   Peter Johnson
Illustration ©   Phillips Fine Art
               Auctioneers
Edited by   Linda Doeser
Designed by   Strange Design Associates

Boxtree Ltd.
36 Tavistock Street
London WC2 7PB

Conceived by Dunestyle Publishing Ltd.

ISBN 1 85283 230 4

Typesetting by O'Reilly Clark, London
Colour separation by J Film Process Co Ltd.,
Bangkok, Thailand
Printed in Italy by New Interlitho spa.

ROYAL
MEMORABILIA

PETER JOHNSON

BOXTREE

Phillips
LONDON

Phillips, founded in 1796, has a reputation for specialisation. Its specialists handle fine art, antiques and collectors' items under more than 60 subject headings — a huge spectrum of art and artefacts that ranges from Old Masters and the finest antique furniture to cigarette cards and comparatively modern pop memorabilia. The auction group's Collectors' Centre, situated at Phillips West Two in Salem Road, Bayswater, London, is constantly recognising, defining and catering for new trends in collecting. It answers hundreds of queries a day from collectors, museums, dealers and the public at large. The shelves of its cataloguing halls are packed with a treasure-trove of objects, awaiting their turn to appear at auction. To varying extents, the scene there and in the main Mayfair salerooms (Phillips, 7 Blenheim Street, London W1Y 0AS; telephone 01-629 6602) is repeated at a score of Phillips branches elsewhere in Britain.

Phillips has the distinction of being the only auction house ever to have held a sale inside Buckingham Palace — in 1836 when the contents of various royal apartments came under the hammer. At the time of the wedding of the Prince and Princess of Wales, while the world wondered about the secrets of Diana's wedding gown, Anne-Marie Benson, head of lace and textiles at Phillips, was called in to advise on the antique lace to be used in the royal parasol, part of the bride's fashion ensemble.

Contents

Chapter 1

Introduction

London Delft plate painted with half-length portraits of William III and Queen Mary, a charming record of their reign at the end of the 17th century, its value in the £400-£600/$640-$960 price bracket; 8½in (21.5cm).

Collecting royal commemorative pottery is a relatively recent phenomenon which has grown rapidly in popularity since the 1960s. The manufacture of china souvenirs relating to contemporary royal events and anniversaries has also become a large and prosperous industry again, for the first time since the inter-war years. This is the result of dramatically increased public and media interest in royalty, particularly British royalty, and, even more, in the new breed of royals with their 'walkabouts', informal television appearances and close personal involvement in public affairs. The Duchess of York pilots a helicopter before our very eyes. Prince Edward, after tentatively treading the boards, embarks on a theatrical career with a humble packet of tea bags in his hand — proof, for those seeking it, of his common touch. The monarch's views on topics once never aired by royalty are known in every home through radio and television.

There is a boom in collecting royal ephemera, clearly demonstrated by the specialized sales which are now part of the regular auction calendar, and by the growth of dealer businesses devoted to the theme. 'Ephemera' is often a misnomer, for although this area of collecting embraces a wealth of paper-based memorabilia, it includes objects of virtue, such as silver photograph frames and other valuable pieces which have belonged to or have had connections with royalty. Nothing could have been less ephemeral than the Duchess of Windsor's jewels, the sale of which, in Geneva in April 1987, was an auction (and social) event of the decade. The story of the jewels, which sold for astronomical

Amid a selection of ware for various monarchs the sad Caroline, consort of George IV, features on the bottom row, right; a pottery dish strongly makes the point that she was 'Her Majesty Caroline, Queen of England'. Such souvenirs of a royal family squabble can still be found for under £100/$160.

prices, is not yet over, nor will it be for a long time while there are still people willing to buy and sell. Nine months after the auction, the press excitedly revealed that a diamond and emerald bracelet, which had belonged to the Duchess, was priced at London's International Silver and Jewellery Fair at a cool £1 million/$1,600,000; trade-watchers recalled it as lot 76 in the 1987 sale, priced then at £217,000/$347,200.

A £1 million royal bauble is sublime, but the game also has its share of the ridiculous. One provincial auction house announced that it had turned down a proffered lot of royal 'memorabilia'. This turned out to be a piece of half-eaten, buttered toast left over from the 1981 wedding breakfast of the Prince and Princess of Wales. 'It would not interest our clients,' was the auctioneer's reply to probing press enquiries.

Million-pound bracelets and buttered toast aside, commemorative china remains the most publicized area of royal collecting. Demand, from American buyers in particular, pushed up values tenfold in the 1980s. Towards the end of the decade, Phillips sold a 900-piece collection belonging to a retired Warwickshire doctor. She had been collecting since 1953 and told *The Independent*, 'In those days commemorative china was sniffed at by smart antique dealers who thought it rather beneath them. Now it has become so sought after they can't get enough of it.' Her collection covered monarchs from Charles II up to the modern times, with the largest section being on Queen Victoria and the latest item a mug celebrating the 1986 wedding of

We know it's Mary, William III's consort, by the initial — otherwise, this rare and naive portrait on an English Delft plate has a delightful 'unisex' look about it; 8½in (21.5cm) and valued in the £1,000-£2,000/$1,600-$3,200 range.

Prince Andew and Sarah Ferguson.

How does a modern issue of a popular commemorative, such as a Prince William birth plate or a Prince Charles 'big ears' wedding mug, reach the collecting charts, where it may rub shoulders with memorabilia of William IV or Edward VII? The process normally takes up to five years. In that time, there will have been sufficient breakages to make surviving examples of the mug rarer than it was at the time of issue. The dustbin syndrome is important in the business of supply and demand; millions of pieces of china have been lost through accident, something which causes no distress at all to shrewd collectors, exulting over the value of their hoards. The next step in the chain is when specialist dealers begin to buy, stock, and sell the mug at a premium. One or two examples may appear, lotted with other specimens, at auction sales of commemoratives. If the object combines quality, appeal and rarity, it may soon start featuring as a single lot. In relatively little time, a £2/$3 souvenir may be priced at ten, then 20 times its original value.

One of the joys of collecting royal commemoratives, whether china or ephemera, is that the antiques of tomorrow are all about us. More than half the trade in this field relates to twentieth-century royalty. Nevertheless, commemoratives of Queen Victoria remain the single most popular theme because of their variety and availability, the rich possibility of finding rarities buried in the mass of commoner material, and the personal charisma of Britain's longest-serving sovereign.

Two handled pottery loving cup, bearing the portraits of George III and Queen Charlotte; on the reverse are portraits of the Prince of Wales and William Pitt. The decoration is blue and orange, and the cup stands 6in (15cm) in height. It is in the £500-£600/$800-$960 class.

Chapter 2

Origins

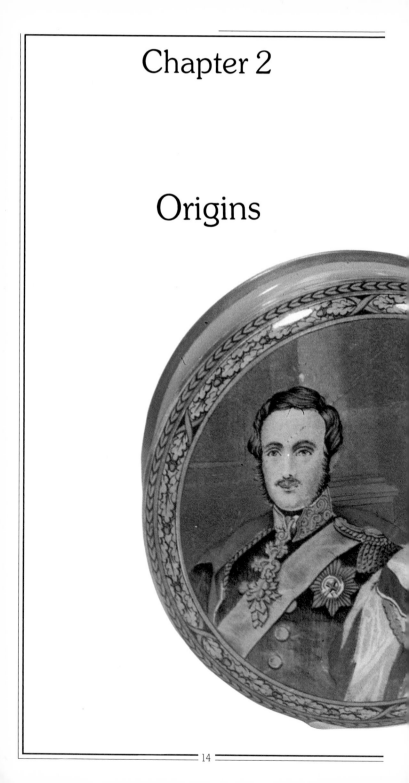

Royalty p14

A late 19th century Staffordshire pot lid showing Victoria and Albert. The pot probably contained a cosmetic compound and sold, together with cover and contents for a matter of pence. Today the lid is in the £150-£200/$240-$320 bracket

Charles II is generally regarded as the first monarch to have had his coronation commemorated on a piece of china. Interestingly, the original picture was meant to be that of Oliver Cromwell and the time-pressed potters of 1660 were able to change only the face. A breakthrough did not come until more than 100 years later, when transfer printing on pottery, as distinct from hand decoration, made mass production possible. Even then, there was no great boom in manufacture. That had to wait until the more affluent Victorian market, with its sophisticated distribution system via railways, canals and roads, and more advanced methods of manufacture.

In the meantime, the troubles of royalty produced some interesting collectors' items. Drinking glasses commemorating the abortive Jacobite rising are among the most expensive examples in the field of glass collecting; a single, rare example may reach several thousand pounds in value. The in-fighting surrounding George III's serious illness in 1789 led to some of the most unusual commemoratives ever made. The monarch's supporters used china as a medium to launch attacks on the enemy and were responsible for ceramic ware which celebrated his recovery.

Later, the marital disharmony of the Prince Regent (later George IV) and Caroline was the target of trenchant comment in commemorative ware. Much of it was sympathetic to the desolate, badly-treated consort whose humiliations are recorded in detail, particularly her being barred access to their daughter. After her husband's succession to the throne, she was engaged in a struggle to be crowned queen.

Homage to the rejected Caroline in a small lustre cream pottery jug, which proclaims: 'Protect my Mother!' and 'God Save Queen Caroline'. About 3in (8cm) in height, and now a collectors' item that would cost £200-£300/$320-$480.

Her supporters produced a flask showing her wearing a crown and the message, 'My hope is in my people'. It is a coveted collectors' piece, worth several hundred pounds. Her death was mourned on plates: 'Tis true our gracious Queen had di'd/ No peace for her on earth was giv'n/ And they on earth a crown deny'd/ We hope she'll wear a crown in heaven.' Her passing was marked in the auction room in a poignant fashion that bordered on the banal: among her possessions to come under the hammer of the ebullient society auctioneer, Harry Phillips, were several thousand bottles of stout.

A surprisingly large variety of china commemoratives of this long-running, royal soap are available to this day and some collectors specialize in them. In scope and volume, however, they pale into insignificance compared with the huge numbers of souvenirs marking the 64-year reign of Queen Victoria, a period which is given detailed attention in later chapters.

After Victoria, her eldest son, Edward VII, holds the palm for commemorative attention (with the exception of modern commemoratives, which are, of course, still being assessed). Almost every event in his life was recorded by the potteries: his birth, christening, engagement, marriage, silver wedding, accession, coronation, birthdays and death. In addition, large quantities of china celebrate official appointments at home and abroad.

On his accession in 1901, the King commissioned half a million beakers from Royal Doulton to be presented to children, the poor and the needy at free dinners to be held throughout London on 5 July, 1902. Called by collectors 'The King's Dinner Beaker', it was

Albert Edward, Prince of Wales (later Edward VII), and the popular Princess Alexandra have their marriage in 1863 celebrated in this pot lid; around £100/$160. It bears the Prince of Wales's feathers and the motto, 'I serve'.

made in green, brown, blue and purple, and each beaker carried the inscription, 'Presented by His Majesty'. Green is the commonest type found today; enthusiasts try to complete a set of four, now worth a few hundred pounds in pristine condition. Peritonitis caused Edward VII's coronation to be postponed from 26 June to 9 August. Most of his coronation commemoratives bear the earlier date, but to some have been added the words, 'Coronation postponed until August 9th'; rarer pieces have the correct date embodied in the design itself.

The reign of George V and Queen Mary produced its quota of commemoratives, ranging from the downright pedestrian, through examples of quirky charm, to rare and well-produced 'cabinet' pieces. This was a routine era for commemoratives much affected by World War I and its aftermath. The interest of collectors is re-awakened by the story of Edward VIII, his love affair with Mrs Simpson and the abdication.

Chapter 3

The China Queen

A George IV and his consort, Caroline, come in for some colourful and decorative treatment in a group of pottery plates dating from around the beginning of the 1820s. They are each in the £100-£200/$160-$320 price bracket.

Jubilees are as old as the civilized world. Their origins were traced in Jubilee Royal, an exhibition organized by the Commemorative Collectors' Society as part of the celebrations to mark Queen Elizabeth II's Silver Jubilee in 1977. The exhibition included a ram's horn trumpet, the Hebrew word for which is *Yobel,* from which the word jubilee derives. (The horn played an important part in the pageantry of Jewish commemorative events). As the exhibition made clear, however, it was during the Victorian era that commemorative items reached the peak of their popularity in Great Britain. Standards of quality inevitably fell as a mass market was indulged, but even the cheapest china items of late Victorian commemorative ware have a charm of their own and an appeal for collectors.

One of the most treasured Victorian pieces is a Swansea purple-transfer mug, marking the young Victoria's coronation in 1838, the year following her accession. It depicts an unfamiliar image of the girlish Queen: her hair is in ringlets and she wears a daring, low-cut dress, presenting an altogether different picture from the later solemn, staid 'mother of empire'. It was far from being a 'one-off' example, but it is usually priced at more than £1,000/$1,600 when it appears at auction, making it one of the most expensive multi-circulation items of royal commemorative china.

At the other end of the scale are mugs and beakers manufactured in large quantities as gifts for schoolchildren from local or central authorities to celebrate royal events. At Derby in 1897, for example, the children received a tin enamel beaker, decorated with colour transfer prints and the worthy sentiment, 'The Queen's

Earliest Resolve — I will be good'. The Mayor of Derby, Sir Thomas Roe, added his name to the beaker's inscription, contained in a framework of designs exuding civic and national aspirations. Buying British, presumably, was not one of these aims; the beakers are marked, 'Made in Austria'.

The Member of Parliament for a Lancashire constituency, Lees Knowles, cemented the allegiance of future voters by presenting a brown, salt-glaze Diamond Jubilee mug to each child of St John's Sunday School, Pendlebury. It was patently a drop in the political ocean, but every vote might have been needed with the zephyrs of change blowing gently through Victorian England as the century

neared its close. The mug bore the inscription, 'Fear God, honour the Queen, remember the 60th year of the reign of Queen Victoria, 1897'. Sunday school evangelism and recruiting zeal must have been high in Pendlebury, as Doulton of Lambeth turned out no fewer than 700 of these mugs for St John's alone.

A celebration of royal commemorative china, ranging from items produced early in Victoria's reign to a decorative mug for the wedding of Prince Charles and Diana.

That production run was nothing compared with the 45,000 Golden Jubilee memorial mugs made by Doulton of Burslem, Staffordshire. The vessel was a slightly tapering, earthenware beaker bearing portraits of Victoria on her accession and as she looked after 50 years' reign. On a June day in 1887 some 30,000 children trooped into London's Hyde Park to receive their mugs from the hands of the Prince of Wales and other dignitaries who had to share the mammoth task of distribution. The children, from board and other elementary schools in London, were given Union Jacks and then formed into columns to receive the royal handout. Although quite a lot of these beakers have survived, collectors regard them as something special — royal commemoratives which owed their being essentially to the patronage of the authorities, rather than straight commercial products. Equally highly regarded is a *de luxe* model in fine white porcelain with gold transfer decoration. This was made for exalted visitors to the Doulton factory.

Some factories revived earlier themes for the Golden Jubilee. Among these were pictures of Prince Albert, Victoria's much mourned consort who had died in 1861, and images of the Queen as

a young woman.

Commemoratives of Prince Albert are treasured, as little was produced at the time of his death. One memento from happier days is a Victoria and Albert wedding plate of 1840, which is valued at several hundred pounds today. Some charming juvenile versions were made as nursery plates at the same time. Compared with the avalanche of china souvenirs of the jubilee, there had been little choice of designs to commemorate events and dates in the early part of the reign. Although a lot of ware was marketed at the time of the coronation, there was little variety, probably because, as a

Mourning rings of black serve to mark the passing of William IV, whose shortish reign received comparatively little commemorative attention against the flood of china that filled the reign of his successor, Queen Victoria. Expect to pay around £200/$320 for a good example.

young princess, Victoria had been kept in seclusion and was little known. A reform flask — a type of liquor container seen in large numbers following the Reform Act of 1832 — even got the young queen's name wrong at the time of the coronation; its inscription refers to her as 'Queen Alexandrina Victoria'.

There was a bewildering range of mottoes on the mugs of 1887.

A Minton porcelain vase produced for the 1947 wedding of Princess Elizabeth and Prince Philip. It was made in a limited edition of 500. In the late 1980s it was changing hands at over £700/$1,120.

'Queen of an Empire on which the sun never sets' was highly popular, and numerous souvenirs sonorously announced, 'Honi soit qui mal y pense'. Patriotism and imperial pride were not in short supply. A salt-glaze stoneware jug of 1897 illustrated Victoria on a medallion and the colonies as shields, with an ostrich as the symbol of Cape Colony, a beaver for Canada, a tiger for India, a

For the same wedding, a two-handled goblet vase from Minton. It is decorated with enamels and gilt.

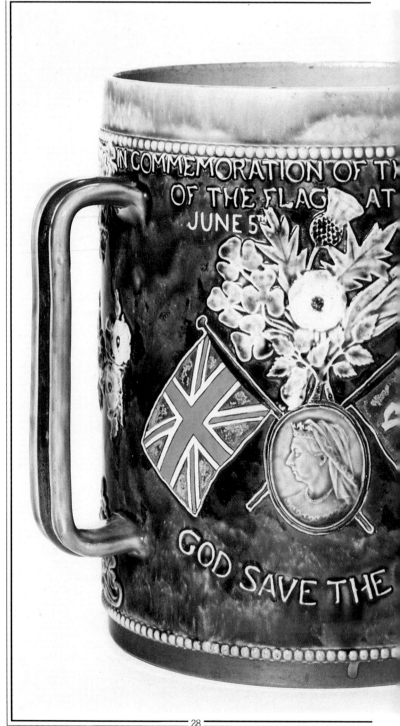

IN COMMEMORATION OF TH
OF THE FLAG AT
JUNE 5

GOD SAVE THE

The Boer war is raging, and the British flag has been raised in Pretoria. Doulton Lambeth celebrates in 1900 with a three-handled loving cup decorated in coloured enamels and bearing Victoria's portrait. A rare item that fetches £300-£400/$480/$640.

kangaroo for Australia and a kiwi for New Zealand. The inscription reads: 'Sons be welded, each and all, into one Imperial whole. One with Britain heart and soul, One life, One flag, One fleet, One throne'.

In an era of Grecian-columned town halls and civic pomposity, it was noticeable how the names of mayors were often printed the same size or larger than the Queen's name on wares handed out to the public. Municipal bigwigs did not necessarily have a monopoly of personalized commemoratives, however.
A little brown jug dating from the Queen's Diamond Jubilee, with portrait, sprays of flowers and ribbon cartouche, boasted an added inscription, 'J. Squire Jun'r., (From Fulham), "Pack Horse". Turnham Green'. Similarly, an earthenware beaker, alive with royal homage, also served to announce that it was 'Presented by Sir William & Lady Grantham on the marriage of Willie & Sybil July 17th, 1897'. Jubilees were for everybody.

Chapter 4

Pomp and Circumstance

Queen Victoria's Golden Jubilee in 1887 and Diamond Jubilee in 1897 produced a massive haul of commemorative items, mainly ceramic, for today's collectors. Objects from her reign are the most popular and widely collected of all royal memorabilia. They represent a collecting field stimulated by the two classic factors of availability and the knowledge that rarities, even ultra rarities, may be lying 'just around the corner'. The decade between the two jubilees provides a convenient watershed; anything later may be categorized as one of tomorrow's antiques, not yet being a century old.

Except to the purely mercenary-minded and some closely blinkered scholars, the social context of objects from the past is important. The true collector wants to know what they tell us of life in those times. He or she is as much interested in discovering contemporary history by reading background ephemera as in the object itself, whether a humble beaker, produced in mass quantities for schoolchildren, or a superb and rare cabinet piece from one of the great factories. A collector specializing in, for example, Victoria's Diamond Jubilee, finds the pages of contemporary newspapers, such as *The*

Illustrated London News and *The Graphic*, fascinating.

At a time when the Queen of Empire could summon as many lavishly accoutred soldiers as she wanted, the nation was thrilled by press accounts of the grand military tattoo held at Windsor Castle on the evening of 19 June 1897. In a scene of splendour, endless lines of Guardsmen held aloft blazing torches to light the ageing queen's view of the proceedings. This was followed by a series of glittering events, such as a state banquet at Buckingham Palace for visiting princes and ambassadors to the Court of St James. The men of empire paraded through London: a naval detachment in straw hats, Indian cavalry plumed and pennanted, exotically uniformed troops from the Pacific islands, African domains and Canada. A troop of New South Wales Lancers from Australia prompted William Britain, the manufacturer of toy soldiers, to rush out a Diamond Jubilee set of lead figures, which he wrongly named the South Australian Lancers, a regiment that did not exist. Despite the mistake, they were a sell-out at 1s 6d (7p/12c) for a box of five. Proving once again that there is nothing like an error to increase collecting value, these are now among the most eagerly

Issued to celebrate the Golden Jubilee of Queen Victoria, this attractive plate was obviously aimed at the Irish market as it is decorated with shamrock.

sought sets of lead soldiers, with a price tag of several hundred pounds.

Jubilee fever affected the representative of *The Illustrated London News,* who was watching the parade. He wrote that the procession was 'heralded by a gay little company of the Royal Horse Guards,' and went on:

'Then, most picturesque of all, came a motley array of infantry, terrible and beautiful to behold — Sikhs, Chinese from Hong Kong, Malays from Singapore, Dyaks, Cingalese, Haussas, West Indian Regiments, Negroes from British Guiana, and dusky warriors from Trinidad, at sight of whom as our allies in hour of peril the colour

JUBILEE YEAR.

COMMENCING JUNE 20TH 1886.

VICTORIA

QUEEN OF GREAT BRITAIN AND IRELAND
EMPRESS OF INDIA.
BORN MAY 24TH 1819.
ASCENDED THE THRONE JUNE 20TH 1837.

distinction was forgotten by even a London crowd . . .'

To open the popular newspapers of the day was to indulge in a feast of jubilation. Advertisements often tell present-day collectors a lot about the collectables that have been handed down from those times. The Queen's profile was blatantly exploited and there was a proliferation of royal puns and

allusions by advertisers.
Spink and Son advertised jubilee
medals for children — 'Lasting
souvenirs. Inexpensive, 100,000
medals ready', No nonsense about
'limited edition' here. Mappin and
Webb, the silversmiths,
trumpeted the qualities of their
'Prince's Plate', which included an
oval biscuit box in plate at £3 3s
(£3.30/$5.28), and in sterling silver
at £10 10s (£10.50/$16,50). A

Victoriana, mainly celebrating or commemorating
the loving marriage between the queen and her
consort, Prince Albert. The Prince Albert memorial
jug depicts him before his monument, the Crystal
Palace. It is in the £200/$320 class today.

manufacturer of fire prevention equipment adopted the slogan, 'Buckingham Palace, Windsor Castle, Osborne House and other Royal Residences have their Merryweather Hand Fire-Pump . . . £5 5s (£5.25/$8.40) complete'. For that sum the buyer obtained bucket, cover, hand pump and hose; a picture showed a gentleman dousing an inferno in the most regal looking of bedrooms.

Another advertisement, itself a collectors' item in showcard form, shouted in bold type: 'Year by year 1837 to 1897 increasing demand for Elliman's Embrocation'. In a nation of animal lovers, the text showed a due sense of priorities, announcing the 'Royal' brand for animals, starting at one shilling (5p/8c), and the 'Universal' brand for humans, starting at 8½d (4p/6c). For humans who wanted to smell a little sweeter, there was 'Queen Victoria's Diamond Bouquet', a

Right Most comprehensive collections of royal commemoratives would include humble tins such as this, produced at the time of Queen Elizabeth's coronation in 1953; worth around £5/$8.

Below left Cheap and cheerful souvenir of the wedding of the Prince and Princess of Wales on June 29, 1981. It usually takes about four years for 'pop' commemoratives to start slowly edging up in value.

Below right The famous Prince Charles 'big ears' mug, a collectors' piece within a short time of its issue in the early 1980s.

A SOUVENIR OF
THE CORONATION OF
H. M. QUEEN ELIZABETH II
1953

scent by Pinaud of Paris, bearing a hardly recognizable image of Her Majesty. There was a 'his and hers' handkerchief set. The lady's handkerchief, 36 cm, (14 in) square, had pierced embroidery edging with the royal cypher, a crown and dates in the corner. The gentleman's was 46 cm (18 in) square and had a wide, royal blue border. However, the real handkerchief bargain of 1887, and still in circulation ten years later, had to be a 56cm (22 in) square of white cotton printed in black, sporting not only pictures of Victoria at the age of ten, at her coronation, wearing a crown and surrounded by her children, visiting a Highland croft, and receiving a visitor from the empire, but also portraits of nine prime ministers who had served during her reign.

Commemorative jewellery came in many forms. Goldsmiths and Silversmiths produced a gold brooch bearing Queen Victoria's

Left A 19th century Baxter card-basket with Queen Victoria in the centre, surrounded by other portraits of royalty and the nobility. Pop art of its day, it is now a collector's piece in the £500/$800 area.

Below Unusual items from Queen Victoria's golden jubilee of 1887: a set of three black-glazed terracotta jugs painted in yellow with portraits, and a similar teapot. In the mid-1980s, such jugs might be found at auction for about £40/$64 apiece, the teapot £70/$112. They have since risen steadily in value.

dates. The public could buy the numerals of the jubilee year 'in diamonds' for £6 10s (£6.50/$10.40) and 'in pearls' for £1 18s (£1.80/$2.88). And, there were jubilee cuff links in heavy gold and bearing the date, for £4($6.40) a pair. Another company undercut this bargain with a nine-carat pair of cuff links, with the head of the younger and the older Victoria on right and left, priced at one guinea (£1.05/$1.68). A shop in Oxford Street·sold a leather purse with lock and date, '37-97', in silver at 10s 6d (51p/82c). The same shop also sold a cased set of six hallmarked teaspoons, depicting busts of the queen on the top and on the bowl — price £1 4s (£1.20/$1.92). One resourceful entrepreneur took space in *The Graphic* to advertise 'Reliable, Dependable, Jubilee Braces'; the carefree spirit might be rife, but there was nothing like being sure.

The crown says it all: an oil-on-copper portrait miniature, after Antonio David, of Prince James Francis Edward, the Old Pretender. A silver-gilt frame studded with rose diamonds bolsters the pretence. The value is around £4,000/$6,400.

Makers of Stevengraphs and other silk pictures had a field day, and there was a torrent of inexpensive prints with royal themes. Most of this jubilee ware was aimed at the working classes, now armed with a new, mass spending power thanks to the advances of the industrial revolution and public education. What was happening, however, at the upper end of the social scale?

At the time of the 50th anniversary celebrations, Queen Victoria's vast family decided on a joint enterprise to give their 'beloved mother and grandmother' an unforgettable jubilee present. It was a magnificent silver, table centrepiece, almost 122 cm (4ft) in length. A large vase stood on a richly chased and engraved silver gilt plateau, its cover bearing raised bosses which displayed the arms of the donors. The vase was

Left Made for the 1902 coronation, these Robinson and Leadbeater white parian busts of Edward VII and Alexandra stand on bronzed metal columns. They are nearly 16in (40cm) in height, and are in the £200/$320 range.

Above A Goss parian bust of Queen Victoria, modelled for Mortlock's of Oxford Street in London. It measures 9in (23cm) in height, and sells for about £200/$320 at auction.

flanked by a lion and a unicorn. Around the base was the inscription: 'To our beloved mother and grandmother Queen Victoria in remembrance of the 50th anniversary of her reign from her children and grandchildren'. The Royal Family, sharing German and British ancestry, had this treasure made in Berlin. Today, it is in the Buckingham Palace collection, which comprises the world's largest and most valuable hoard of royal memorabilia.

Chapter 5

Abdication Confusion

'A pretty kettle of fish' is how Queen Mary is said to have described the constitutional, political and family complications arising from her son's wish to marry the American divorcee, Wallis Simpson. Collectors of commemoratives might be forgiven for borrowing the royal epithet to describe the muddle left in the wake of Edward VIII's abdication on 10 December, 1936. The current state of confusion, compounded by commercial panic and opportunism in equal parts, resulted from the chaos into which the souvenir industry had been plunged.

Far left Sketches by Victorian royalty often come on the collector market. This delightful 19th century watercolour and pencil work by Victoria Princess Royal is of one of the royal children and worth about £300/$480.

Below Another from the sketch album of Victoria Princess Royal; the woman could be a servant, the child probably a member of the royal family; £200/$320-plus.

'I have an Edward VIII coronation mug. It must be rare because the coronation never took place.' This hopeful refrain is familiar to every auction house, specialist dealer and general trader in collectables. Edward VIII did, of course, give up his throne some six months before he was due to crowned, but the British and export markets were already flooded with commemorative china and other objects from an industry well prepared for the expected big event of 1937. Consequently, there is no scarcity of coronation commemoratives.

From his early youth, he had been a popular subject for the souvenir makers. As a three-year-old, he played his part in Queen Victoria's Diamond Jubilee of 1897 by appearing on some plates, tins and handkerchiefs. He featured on commemoratives produced for the coronations of his grandfather, Edward VII, and his father, George V. There are items dating from his investiture as Prince of Wales at Caernarvon in 1911.

These usually showed him in midshipman's uniform. Some items were concerned exclusively with the investiture, while others also included transfers and motifs produced for his parents' coronation in the same year. A crested Parian ware figure of the Prince, marking his visits to the trenches of the Western Front was produced during World War I, and his 21st birthday in 1915 has left a printed tin tea-caddy

esteemed by collectors.

From the 1920s onwards, his exposure and popularity increased, helped by tours of industrial and economically distressed areas of Britain and well publicized voyages abroad. There are mugs and plates commemorating his good works; those related to industrial tours were usually produced for local schoolchildren.

When George V died on 21

Celebrating the 1839 wedding of the Duke of York and Princess May, later to become King George V and Queen Mary, this mug and fluted bowl are fairly inexpensive commemoratives, in the under £50/$80 class.

Fairies too have their royalty. This superb Doulton
Lambeth faience tile panel was created by
Margaret E. Thompson. 'Sleeping Beauty — The
Fairies at the Christening' sold at Phillips in 1986
for £4,000/$6,400.

January, 1936, Edward VIII came to the throne. By the end of the year, he had abdicated because he wanted to make a constitutionally unacceptable marriage to a twice-divorced woman. Rita Smythe, whose London business, Britannia, trades in large quantities of royal mementoes, sums up the scene left by the abdication: 'The fact that Edward was never crowned leads to delusions of rarity. At the time of the abdication the warehouses and stores were stuffed with tens of thousands of cheap pottery mugs in a multitude of designs, waiting for Edward's coronation. Today they are worth just a bit more than the corresponding ones for George VI and Elizabeth.' (Since these comments were made, the sale of the Duchess of Windsor's jewels in 1987 has refuelled interest in everything related to the story of the abdication and so marginally increased the value of coronation china of Edward VIII.)

However, Mrs Smythe maintains that is not the whole story. Many factories were working rather more slowly on better quality pieces, and some of these are still around. The production runs were halted and lines were finished almost as soon as they started. In some cases, they were smashed up as worthless — and perhaps a few got away. 'At the Minton factory,' Mrs Smythe explains, 'a superb beaker in a fitted wooden box was being made in a limited edition of 2,000. It is not known how far they got (three-figure numberings are not frequent) but all the finished pieces were given away to the staff. Today the price is well into three figures. These are the Edward items worth looking for, the bone china pieces, well enamelled and gilded — and there is a surprising variety, in small quantities.'

The Commemorative Collectors' Society has documented more than 400 separate designs of main souvenirs issued for the coronation of Edward VIII. By far the largest section — some 140 designs — relates to mugs, with books a close second. In the list are plates, jugs, vases, bowls, metal and ceramic wall plaques, handkerchiefs, flags, printed tin

The large wall plate, in colours and gilded, is a Maling souvenir of Edward VIII, probably with inscriptions added or altered after his abdication in 1936; 12½in (31cm), £100-£150/$160-$240. The smaller wall plate by Royal Worcester was issued for the coronation of his brother, King George VI, in 1937; under £100/$160. Stranger in the group is a loving cup saluting heroes of the Crimean War.

boxes, tin trays, special magazines
and ceramic and metal busts.
In addition, there are beakers,
cups and saucers, teasets and fine
ornamental glass and china,
ash-trays, tea caddies, toys,
games, jigsaw puzzles,
money-boxes, postcards, paper
napkins, playing cards, paper
carrier bags, lapel buttons, pens
and pencils.

Some children's mugs were
made in blue for a boy and pink
for a girl. A rare earthenware

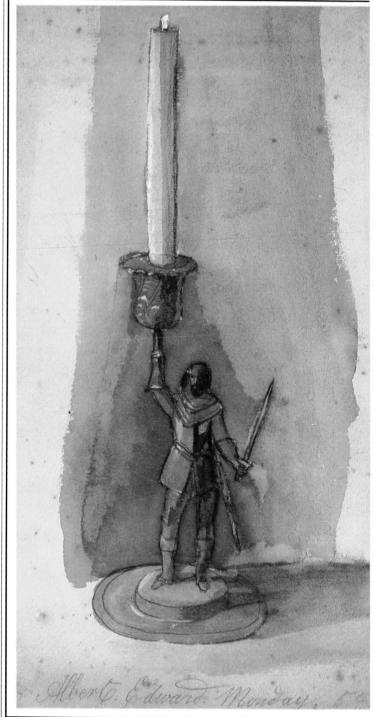

Albert. Edward. Monday.

beaker shows a youthful looking king actually wearing his crown. For the most part, these things were sold as rather wry, possibly poignant, souvenirs of a crowning that never happened and many because cherished personal mementoes of living history which people could see being made every day in the newspaper headlines.

However, what were the factories to do with the stocks of commemoratives left on their shelves? Many glass items were broken up for re-use. The potteries however, had to improvise or start again on commemoratives of the new King — and his Queen, Elizabeth, who through a long life was to become the most loved royal personality of the century. Edward's younger brother, the Duke of York, was crowned King George VI on 12 May, 1937. This date had originally been set for Edward's coronation and was a small and welcome mercy for the commercial manufacturers desperately experimenting with exchanged transfers of inscription and image in an effort to recoup some of their losses. Collectors revere a good-quality earthenware mug by Wilkinson, the design of which was commissioned from Dame Laura Knight by the British Pottery Manufacturers' Federation in an effort to raise the standard of souvenirs. The mug, prominently featuring Edward's head, is unusual in that the manufacturer resourcefully applied additional transfers and turned it into a coronation/abdication piece. The word 'proposed' was added to read 'Proposed Coronation King Edward VIII', and the inscription 'Abdicated Dec 10th 1936' was hastily added around the rim.

Other china souvenirs bear the

The Prince of Wales, later Edward VII, sketched this candlestick in pencil and watercolour and signed it; £200-plus/$320-plus.

The date was May 12, 1937. Edward VIII should have been crowned. On that date, however, his brother was crowned instead, Edward having abdicated. The Paragon porcelain loving cup was made for Edward's coronation; it is today worth a value of around £200-£300/$320-$480. The jug of almost a century earlier shows the young Victoria reviewing her troops; it heads now towards a £500/$800 figure.

contradiction 'Long May He Reign' on the front and 'Abdicated 10 December 1936' on the back. The abdication 'stop-press' news was added to a musical jug by Fielding which plays 'Here's a Health Unto His Majesty', a cabinet piece of distinction for any collector. In their desire to adapt existing designs, some makers squeezed in two heads where one had been before; others stretched the design to make room for the extra portrait of

King George. Collectors of Britain's lead soldiers pay twice as much for a coronation coach carrying Edward VIII, his robes spread voluminously across the entire seat, as for a later model, produced over the years in large quantities, containing both George VI and Queen Elizabeth side by side. In an excess of improvisation, one manufacturer used up spare transfers from the 1935 Jubilee of George V and the cancelled Edward VIII coronation, and combined them with a new one for George VI's crowning, all on one mug, and called it 'The Three Kings of 1936'.

As a general rule, altered coronation mugs are worth half as much again as those from the original batch, but this varies according to type and rarity. A few mugs were made specially to mark the abdication, sometimes including a part of the King's

A postcard worth many hundreds of pounds, this colourful souvenir of Edward VII's coronation in 1902 was dropped from a balloon over Kent. It depicts previous kings called Edward and came 'with love to all from Hilda & Chris'.

moving speech to the nation over the radio. These are keenly sought by enthusiasts. One company which obviously found it difficult to clear even the abdication mugs, added further words and the date to mark the wedding of the newly created Duke of Windsor on 3 June, 1937.

The expatriate former king subsequently featured on a small number of commemoratives, although the books and articles on 'the love affair of the century' would fill an archive. There is a postal cover for the day of his wedding at Monts in France, bearing an oval photograph of the couple. The bride is described oddly as 'Mrs Wallis Warfield', the surname being her maiden name. A couple of unremarkable commemoratives were produced at the Duke's death in Paris on

*Left*George IV beaker, Edward VIII three-handled loving cup and an Edward beaker. The Minton beakers are in the near-£100/$160 class, the loving cup by Spode is worth £300-£400/$480-$640.

Below A mixed bag of 20th century items which would form the nucleus of a respectable collection. It is dominated by an Aynsley 'Jubilee Vase' issued in 1977 to mark the 25th anniversary of Queen Elizabeth II's accession. A decade after the jubilee, the vase was changing hands at about £350-£400/$560-$640.

28 May, 1972, described by Rita Smythe as 'a Coalport plate of restrained design, and a tankard with lamentably amateurish portraits of the Duke and Duchess.'

The myth of the scarcity of Edward VIII memorabilia lingers on, however, as the following postscript demonstrates. In the early 1980s, an article appeared in an American antiques magazine under the headline, 'The one that got away'. It described how an Edward VIII coronation mug by Shelley pottery was sent to South Africa well before the proposed coronation and so escaped being scrapped with the other memorabilia designed for the occasion. The author suggested that it was one of only two survivors, the other being presented to someone personally by the Duke of Windsor at a later date. 'Factories were required to destroy all existing memorabilia under the eye of royal inspectors, and everything so destroyed was invoiced and paid for by the Crown,' the American magazine reported. Alas, the magazine was no better informed on the scarcity of Shelley mugs than it was on the powers possessed by the Crown and its 'inspectors'.

For a time in the early 1980s this was the world's most expensive airmail at more than £1,000/$1,600. It is another balloon-drop card for Edward VII's coronation — 'this is a new method of posting...'.

BECKENHAM .
CELEBRATION.

Long live our sovereigns,
England's King and Queen!

INDIA

NEW ZEALAND

CORONATION
SOUVENIR
1902

VII

CAPE

AUSTRALIA

CANADA

Despatched from the Clouds by Balloon Post,
Coronation Day, Aug. 9th, 1902.

Raphael Tuck & Sons "Coronation" Postcard Series 608 II.
Designed in England Chromographed in Bavaria.

Dearest Lux - this is a new method of posting - I hope you will like this card to add to your collection. yours.

The power and function of royalty can be a hazy area for those who live in countries where it is not enshrined in the constitution. Myth and romance are mingled with fact and, indeed, such attributes help create an air of glamour and mystery which in itself adds to the subject's interest. Overseas collectors of royal memorabilia may sometimes be susceptible to myth, especially when it fuels their enjoyment of collecting. But such a situation may lead to traps for the unwary, as the magazine *Antique Collecting* (the journal of the British Antique Collector's Club) pointed out in an examination of the Shelley mug affair. It published a letter written to the offending editor by Steven Jackson, secretary of the Commemorative Collectors' Society, in which he observed:

'Whilst the story of how this particular mug found its way to South Africa is most interesting, many of the statements made in the article are inaccurate and perpetuate the myth that such items for this particular coronation are rare or in some way unique and unusual.

'Commemorative items for royal events are, and always have been, a purely commercial venture and may be produced by anyone anywhere. In addition to ceramic mugs and plates etc, they also appear as printed tin boxes and trays, enamel mugs, printed and woven fabrics, pressed and engraved glass, and souvenir books and magazines, etc. Factories were never and are not "instructed to manufacture a coronation mug" and Shelley did not receive "orders to produce the commemoratives" in the context that statement implies.

'Far more misleading, however, is the statement that "Factories were required to destroy all existing memorabilia under the eye of royal inspectors, and everything so destroyed was invoiced to and paid for by the Crown". This is just simply not true — the government of the day or the Crown have no legal right, or indeed any wish, to interfere in what is a private commercial activity. Many newspapers at the time of the abdication openly reported that shops were doing a brisk trade in items for the coronation of the king who was never crowned, and a great many of these items have survived to this day and are still quite easily available.'

After referring to the large variety of designs produced for Edward VIII's coronation and the numbers of items with altered inscriptions, Jackson went on: 'We also regret to say that the Shelley mug illustrated in the article is quite common and, in addition to the mug, a matching plate, vase and bowl were also issued by the same factory. What is so unfortunate and why we are so concerned about this article is that a great many sincere new collectors are misled by this information, and may be tempted to pay a high price for an item for Edward VIII's coronation, only to learn at a later date that such pieces are quite common and relatively cheap to buy either from dealers or at auction where they come up for sale quite frequently.'

Chapter 6

A Matter of Taste

An unusual souvenir of the present Prince of Wales's wedding celebrations hangs on the kitchen wall of a modest collector of modern royal memorabilia. A humble example of the torrent of artefacts that marked the occasion, it is, nevertheless, regarded with affection by the collector and her family. It is a heart-shaped ginger bread biscuit, some 25 cm (10 in) at its widest, with coloured icing which traces ribbon decoration and the names of the couple. A hole near the top allows the heart to be hung up, and the whole thing is securely encased by the clear plastic wrapper in which it was sold in 1981.

I have not come across any record of this culinary love token in lists of royal memorabilia issues or in auction catalogues and know of its existence only through a dinner-party conversation with the collector's sister. Nevertheless, it is a valid item of royal memorabilia, a 'fun' piece of *kitsch*, and a scarce collectable whose rarity depends on the premise that most of its fellows have been eaten!

At the time of the wedding, the editor of *Art & Antiques Weekly* voiced her opinion on taste and vulgarity: 'What is it about royal events that apparently causes such a drying-up of the creative

juices? The symbols of royalty never change — but is it really necessary to incorporate them into every design? Heraldic devices, coronets and Prince of Wales feathers are all very well — but when exploited in such profusion they quickly become very boring . . . Disappointingly, when a company does manage to dream up something out of the ordinary, more often than not it's just plain vulgar.'

The edible heart may have been vulgar, but in its day it had at least the merit of cheapness. That can hardly be said of another, more 'up-market', wedding souvenir which was announced as a 'brilliant fantasy from our leading silversmith' and was entitled the Surprise Mushrooms. They came in a pair, one with silvered top, the other gilded, standing on a slate base. Read on: 'Lift the top of each Mushroom, and one finds the Woodland Folk preparing the regalia for "The Day". The Pixie is putting together the ostrich feathers; the Fairy is completing her herald crest . . .' The 1981 price for this horror was £295/$472. It would also be interesting to know how the Wilkinson Royal Wedding Sword, in a limited edition of 1,000, fared: hilt with twin knuckle bows bearing the full Christian names of the royal couple, ceremonial dress knot of

Dating from her wedding in 1922, this simple pottery mug is decorated in brown and gilt with a portrait of Lady Elizabeth Bowes-Lyon. Her popularity, first as the mother of the little princesses, then as the consort of George VI, later still as the Queen Mother, underwrites its collector value: it is a rare piece, well over £100/$160.

Right Queen Alexandra, wife of Edward VII, featured in a Taddy's series of Royalty cigarette cards in 1903. A far from rare set, a full house of 25 is nearing the £100/$160 mark.

Below Royalty, Actresses and Soldiers — that was the eclectic theme of this set of 20 Taddy's cigarette cards of 1898. The Prince of Wales found himself among some of his European cousins. In 1987 the set sold at auction for £2,420/$3,872.

Below right War in the east in 1904 gave Taddy's the excuse to introduce a Russo-Japanese series of cigarette cards (the 50 are in the £200-£300/ $320-$480 bracket). Here is number 14, 'Emperor of Russia'.

14   EMPEROR OF RUSSIA

"Royalty" Series N° ?

Her Majesty The Queen.

silver-plated thread, affixed to the guard, and special brackets for wall-hanging. The price was £450/$720. What we do know is that the infamous Prince Charles 'big-ears' mug (with a giant ear forming the handle) was a hot seller in general stores, and remains so today in different role — as a collectors' item, changing hands in the antique markets at many times its early 1980s value.

The collector of royal *kitsch,* who possesses the jolly kit issued at the time of the wedding by Woody Enterprises of Birmingham, is fortunate. The clear plastic package annouces: 'Be a Royal Chauffeur'. It contains a life-sized colour photograph of Prince Charles, and behind, peeping out, is the Princess of Wales. There are two life-sized hands, his and hers. The instructions attached to the kit (£4.60/$7.36 in 1981) are clear: '1. Ensure [car] window is clean, dry and free from grease. 2. Peel off adhesive cover. 3. Press firmly on to inside of windows'. The photographs give the impression to an onlooker, at least for a fleeting instant, that you are chauffering the royal couple. The illusion is helped by the hands, attached to the cuffs by strips of springy metal, so that they vibrate as though waving when the car is in motion. The car package and 'big-ears' mug stand out among the lighter-hearted examples of royal wedding memorabilia.

Steven Jackson, of the Commemorative Collectors' Society, has said: 'Choice is determined by emotive impulse. Commemoratives by their very nature are mass-produced items and very few have artistic merit.' Rosemary Prior, of the Sussex Commemorative Ware Centre, wrote at the time of the wedding: 'There are many different opinions on what is collectable or not, which is just as well since all tastes must be catered for'.

It has been a long haul for royal commemoratives from solemn and respectful images of the young Queen Victoria to irreverent lampooning of the heir to the throne. The process, particularly in relation to ceramics and similar wares, found a natural watershed in World War II, and post-war souvenirs are a study of their own.

China fairings were made mainly in Germany and usually had jokey themes, popular with late-Victorian society; they sold in trinket shops and on fairgrounds. This uncharacteristically serious fairing of large size (7in — 18cm) depicts the emperor Franz Josef in full regalia. It is in the £100-£200/$160-$320 class.

A porcelain figure of Frederick the Great, standing
on a mahogany base, one of the finest models to
come from the short-lived Allach factory.

Chapter 7

In the Public Eye

When George VI came to the throne in 1937, he was not used to the limelight. Thrust into the glare of public scrutiny (which was soon to become intense, as he and his consort shared the vicissitudes of war with their subjects), he constantly and bravely fought to conquer an inherent shyness, that was exacerbated in those radio-conscious days by a speech defect. Before Edward VIII's abdication, the Duke and Duchess of York had lived a life of relative obscurity, performing their official duties modestly and efficiently and having little impact on the media. The commemorative industry devoted little attention to the couple, compared with the tributes accorded to the more glamorous Edward, Prince of Wales.

Lady Elizabeth Bowes-Lyon who, as the Queen Mother, was to develop into a royal megastar, was hardly known to the general public at the time of her wedding in 1923. The wedding, a splendid, formal affair in Westminster Abbey and the focus of much press attention, is commemorated in few collectables, Ian and Rita Smythe, the London dealers in commemoratives, observe: 'The only designs to remind us of it now are four or five tins, a pair of pin-dishes and some strange aluminium beakers. All this could

be comfortably packed into a carrier-bag with everything that was done for the Duke of Kent's wedding to Princess Marina 11 years later. Where was everybody?'

With the 1937 coronation, however, royal souvenirs of King George and Queen Elizabeth came to the forefront. Wartime and post-war austerity were later to affect the output of commemoratives associated with their elder daughter, Princess Elizabeth, but in the meantime, the heir presumptive and her younger sister, Margaret, enjoyed a rapturous wave of public popularity which can be seen from the wealth of royal memorabilia. Their births, in 1926 and 1930 respectviely, had been marked with china collectables. From 1937, they frequently appeared on mugs, beakers and plates, together with their newly crowned parents. Often they enjoyed the attention on their own. The Paragon China Company rang the changes. Its royal coffee and tea service featured two magpies sitting on blossomed boughs, entitled 'Two for Joy' for Princess Elizabeth, and green and yellow budgerigars in similar salutation for Princess Margaret. When the description on a souvenir is 'Princess Elizabeth of York' the piece was made before

Romance in lead: Prince Charles, the Prince of Wales, in red-jacketed mess uniform, with a glamorously gowned Princess of Wales, as made by the British toy soldier manufacturer, Blenheim.

King George ascended the throne; afterwards, she was usually described as 'The Princess Elizabeth'.

War halted the large-scale manufacture of commemoratives, and royal souvenirs of this period tend to come under the classification of ephemera — signed photographs, greetings cards and so on. Treasured images include the King and Queen, talking to fellow Londoners amid the rubble of the blitz and inspecting a bombed wing of Buckingham Palace; the royals with a siren-suited Winston Churchill; or Princess Elizabeth, wearing the khaki dungarees of the auxiliary service, 'doing her bit' for Britian.

Compared with the flood of commemoratives which greeted the wedding of Prince Charles and Lady Diana 34 years later, **there was little to mark the marriage in 1947 of Princess Elizabeth to Lieutenant Philip Mountbattan, the newly created Duke of Edinburgh. Rationing was** still in force and the potteries had not yet recovered from the effects of the war as they geared up to new times in a climate of shortages and difficulties. In the same year, Heals of London commissioned a plate to record the royal family's visit to South Africa, but the few good commemoratives produced by British industry were mainly earmarked for export.

Popular souvenirs of the royal wedding were limited to brooches, lapel badges, mirrors and small compacts, a glass tumbler and a somewhat crude pottery mug issued by the Euwenny Pottery in Wales. Scarcity gives some of these artefacts a value far beyond the level of their quality. A more ambitious production, a Royal Worcester figure of Elizabeth on

Above A poured-wax figure of Queen Victoria, nearly 20in (48cm) in height. Her sombre look and black mourning dress probably indicate that the figure was not meant as a child's doll — more likely something to stand on a Victorian parlour sideboard.

Below In the world of lead soldiers, the figures of Richard Courtenay, a 20th century maker, are aristocrats. These little finger-sized models represent Henry VIII, Catherine of Aragon and Cardinal Wolsey.

Bottom A superb Richard Courtenay model of Henry V, a conqueror among lead soldiers. Mounted figures of named royalty such as this frequently sell for over £200/$320 apiece when they appear in the auction lists.

horseback, as at Trooping the Colour, was issued in an edition of 100. Rarity has imbued it with desirability, but the equestrian figure's fortunes have had a bumpy ride: in the late 1960s, an example was said to have sold for £15,000/$24,000; nearly 20 years later, specialist dealers were quoting a figure of £5,000-£6,000/$8,000-$9,600. It would be difficult to chart the market for such a maverick performer.

Collectors report an absolute dearth of items to mark the death of George VI in 1952. Rosemary Prior, of the Sussex Commemorative Ware Centre, sent out a warning in 1981 about certain, straight-sided earthenware mugs depicting a full-length figure of George VI in uniform, which purport to have been made in his memory in 1952: 'Beware! These reproductions, made recently "to fill a gap" — something we frown on very strongly and something, I am happy to say, that does not happen often to commemoratives.'

The souvenir industry began to gather momentum for Elizabeth II's coronation in 1953, but it reached nothing approaching top gear until 1969 with the investiture of Prince Charles as Prince of Wales. A Royal Crown Derby coronation loving cup, in limited edition, cost about £12/$19.20 in 1953; it had appreciated tenfold by the early 1980s, and by even more since. Coronation items can be formal: a Tuscan bone china plate pays homage to the Queen depicted wearing a tiara, and draws heavily on Victorian tradition. They can be informal, too: a popular 1953 piece is a mug with a Marcus Adams portrait of the Queen in relaxed mood, together with the young Prince Charles and Princess Anne. The same picture appears on cup, saucer and teaplate, and these are popular collectors' items today, largely thanks to the inclusion of the royal children.

During the late 1960s and early

Royalty in the toy cupboard: lead figures of Louis XV of France, with his wife, mistress and mother, a gentleman and guards; by Vertunni, a celebrated maker of model soldiers for connoisseurs. The group is worth about £200/$320.

ROYAL WEDDING EXHIBITION

A PRINCESS FOR WALES

T.R.H. The Prince and Princess of Wales 1863

An Exhibition
organised by
The
Commemorative
Collectors
Society

In association with
THE OBSERVER
at
The Guildhall Windsor
20th July - 8th August
1981

£2   SOUVENIR CATALOGUE   £2

1970s, a new generation of royals was making news. In Britain, as in other European countries which had retained their monarchies, this new young breed enjoyed a freedom unheard of in the days of their parents and grandparents. The international gossip and camera brigades were attracted to the *nouvelle vague* of liberated royalty like flies to honey. Furthermore, the 30th anniversary of Edward VIII's abdication had been met by an avalanche of print, recalling 'the greatest love story of the century'. Former employees were tempted by the prospect of down-payments or fat royalties to loosen their tongues about their royal masters and mistresses and their private lives inside the hitherto closed palaces and castles. Tomes on royal topics burst into the best seller lists.

The precedent had been set, in a fairly decorous manner, in 1950, when Marion Crawford, governess to the Princesses Elizabeth and Margaret for 17 years, published her memoirs, *The Little Princesses.* Her story was the first of a number of 'saccharine commentaries in books and articles on the same theme, and which have since become legion,' as *The Times* put it. The memoirs of 'Crawfie', as the Princesses called her and as millions came to know her, were first published in the United States in *Ladies' Home Journal*, and in Britain, *Woman's Own* quickly followed suit. 'Here is a warm affectionate account of a happy family in their everyday lives, told against a background of momentous events in history,' explained the advertising blurb. The British press rose in indignation — and simultaneously scurried to publish the more exciting snippets of Crawfie's remembrances.

Top left The 1933 signature of the Prince of Wales, later Edward VIII. All things to do with Edward have become keenly collected — especially memorabilia dating from the abdication period and afterwards.

Bottom left The printed ephemera of royalty is eagerly collected. Here is a souvenir catalogue of an exhibition organised by the Commemorative Collectors Society for the 1981 wedding of the Prince and Princess of Wales. It has become a collectors' item in itself.

'At the same time, however, her revelations, many of them innocuous in comparison to the published inanities of today's "royal watchers", both scandalised and delighted; the Court, and Establishment opinion generally, considered the exercise to be vulgar and a breach of trust,' observed a *Times* obituary writer, recording the death of Crawfie in February 1988. The former governess 'revealed', for example, that the young Princesses had been besotted by horses. They had a 'stable' of 30 toy horses which were carefully tended and unsaddled each night. Crawfie herself was frequently harnessed and had to prance around, while 'Lilibet' pretended to deliver the groceries. Such snippets of trivia helped to fuel public fascination with royalty, and stimulated a corps of nascent royal watchers to seek, embroider or manufacture similar, highly saleable anecdotes. It was inevitable that the surge of frenetic activity by the international *papparazzi*, which both reflected and created public interest, should find a parallel in the royal commemorative industry. The depiction of royalty had become a lucrative business.

Princess Margaret's wedding in 1960 brought an upturn in output, but it was the investiture of the Prince of Wales at the end of the Swinging Sixties that marked a new starting point. It has left us a wealth of commemoratives, both those with mass appeal — the cheerful 'cheapies' that should have their place in any definitive collection — and the expensive variety of top-quality china from well-known factories.

At the time of Queen Elizabeth II's Silver Jubilee in 1977, the Commemorative Collectors' Society estimated that £12.5

A very fine collection of 26 Russian dolls' house dolls, representing the royal family, smuggled out of Russia at the time of the Revolution by a young English girl. In the mid-1980s, these sold at auction for nearly £3,000/$4,800.

million/$20 million worth of jubilee souvenirs would be sold that year, and its chairman, Sir Lincoln Hallinan, was quoted as saying that most of those souvenirs were 'dull, unimaginative and pedestrian'. However, a glance through *Jubilee Royal*, the catalogue of the society's special exhibition of souvenirs, proves that many were certainly up to or surpassed the standards of artefacts from previous royal jubilees.

Apart from expensive, high-quality items, the following objects surely deserve to be enshrined in the collections of those who possess a sense of balance. An earthenware mug designed by the Royal College of Art is decorated with borders of mice dressed in ermine cloaks and wearing crowns, and an inscription reads: 'We are the royal mice, and we thought it

Royalty for the richest. King Henry VIII by Hans Holbein the Younger, painted on an oak panel and dating probably from a time not long after the beheading of Anne Boleyn on May 19, 1536. Old Master Paintings from the Thyssen-Bornemisza Collection, an exhibition presented by the Royal Academy and *The Times*, March 1988.

would be rather nice . . .' A plate and beaker commissioned by a merchant in Tonga combines a portrait of Queen Elizabeth II and King Topou IV. (Some of these mugs are by now much-travelled and have appeared at auctions in London.) A plate exported to Australia boasts koala bears and merino sheep with sprays of Australian flowers. The jubilee shopper could dress up in an array of patriotic and loyal items of clothing, from socks and singlets to T-shirts and headscarfs, not to say a range of lacy underwear.

Four years after the Jubilee, during the celebrations of Prince Charles's wedding, the debate about standards and quality took place again in the national and collector press. More esoteric items, such as the Prince Charles 'big-ears' mug and a cardboard royal couple to travel in the back seats of your car, are discussed in Chapter 6 *A Matter of Taste*. Most collectors will agree that the Victorians and their forbears had no monopoly of good taste. Many commemorative items produced in the 20th century will stand the test of time. Events in the lives of the Princes William and Harry (their birth commemoratives have already started to be collected) and other royal children will be celebrated in increasingly interesting ways. The trend is towards affectionate irreverence mixed with the traditional respect and homage.

Chapter 8

Ephemera Royal

A minor treasure was discovered during the centenary celebrations of Boots the Chemist Ltd in 1977, and this coincided happily with Queen Elizabeth's Silver Jubilee that year. It has also added a previously unknown item to the lists of royal ephemera. The find is now enshrined in the official Boots archive at Nottingham, along with the elixirs, compounds and potions that tell the story of Jesse Boot and his heirs. The provident celebrant who braved the rigours of the 1937 coronation, with its nocturnal merrymaking in the streets of London and the long wait for the procession on the big day, just had to have a Boots pocket 'Emergency Set'. These were most probably manufactured for Edward VIII's coronation, but were equally serviceable when George VI was crowned instead. Packed in a neat, red, tin box, the kit consists of aspirin, eau de cologne, lavender smelling-tubes and a bottle labelled, 'The Carminative Stimulating Draught — Ready to drink — half the contents of this bottle should be taken slowly as a pick-me-up'.

Today's collector might wrily observe that such an emergency set would be useful on viewing days at a specialized auction of royal ephemera, when a huge and bewildering choice of objects is on offer. These may range from a Georgian autographed note from the 18th century, to modern Xeroxed instructions from the Palace for accredited press photographers covering a 'Fergie and Andrew' expedition in the Canadian backwoods. There is usually an equally wide variety of subject matter and royal personages: Christmas cards signed by the Queen Mother in the 1960s (averaging about £60/$96 apiece in the late 1980s), a silver-framed and inscribed portrait of Grand Duke Michael, grandson of Tsar Nicholas I (£300/$460), and signed photographs of King Saud and Crown Prince Fahd of Saudi Arabia (estimated at £30/$48 and, in the event, lacking a bidder).

The growth of collecting in recent years has prompted auction houses and dealers to separate royal ephemera from 'commemoratives', the latter meaning mainly ceramic souvenirs or related items. There are special sales for the different types of items. The days are gone when the Waterman desk fountain-pen with which Edward VIII signed the abdication document can crop up in a general sale, as it did during the 1970s. It realized the then considerable sum of £2,000/$3,200. If it were to reappear today, it would be given a prominent

Magnificent silver frames helped lift the auction price of this pair of signed photographs of King George VI and Queen Elizabeth to nearly £4,000/$6,400.

position in a specialized auction of royal ephemera, and its price would accordingly be much higher, particularly in the light of enhanced interest in everything to do with the Windsors.

Even a simple pencil autograph of Edward, when Prince of Wales, can fetch £20-£30/$32-$48. When the autograph letter contains 'quotes' of interest, the value rises. Prices of £200-£300/$320-$480 have been paid for individual letters in a series written by Edward VIII to his equerry shortly before and during the World War I. His observations are much

prized by the collector or biographer: 'I am longing to go to India to kill a tiger . . .' 'The [cigarette] holder is a most useful one and prevents the nicotine going down one's throat. I shall always use it . . .' 'There is [at Oxford] absolutely no snobbishness and everyone knows everyone else. The former vice is very rife in other places . . .' 'I do envy him [his brother] this ripping cruise in the Mediterranean . . .' 'Those Germans are getting it in the neck thank goodness!!' 'This is a most rotten war unless you are actually

Making free with royal patronage. Parkins & Cotto, court stationers, maximise the value of their connections with the new Queen Alexandra — an advertisement in a special five-shilling 'record' number of *The Illustrated London News*, issued to salute the reign of Queen Victoria.

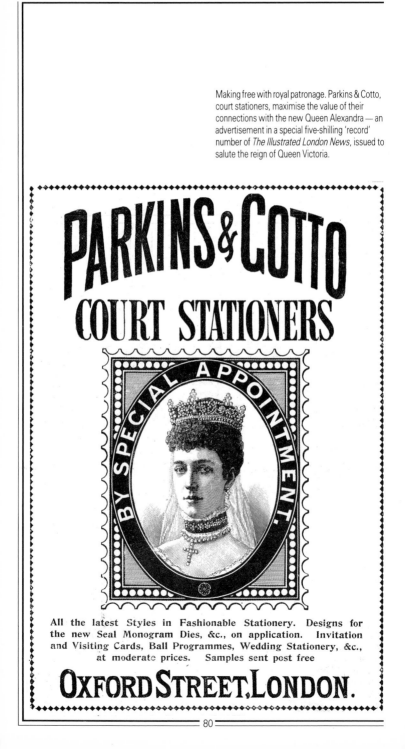

PARKINS & COTTO
COURT STATIONERS

BY SPECIAL APPOINTMENT.

All the latest Styles in Fashionable Stationery. Designs for the new Seal Monogram Dies, &c., on application. Invitation and Visiting Cards, Ball Programmes, Wedding Stationery, &c., at moderate prices. Samples sent post free

OXFORD STREET, LONDON.

fighting!!' '[Thanks for] good wishes for my rotten birthday which was a sad event this year with this bloody war on and so many of one's best friend's killed . . .' '. . . that Zeppelin raid, what a triumph if we had brought one of the buggers down in Hyde Park!!' 'What a splendid thing abolishing the Hun names in my family . . .'. And, on the subject of a richly disliked governess in the royal household, '. . . that dreadful woman Dussau, whom Bertie and I find it hard to refrain from poisoning when we are at home . . .'

If an item is related to the love affair, abdication and the long sequel, the value rises dramatically. An envelope addressed to Mrs E. Simpson, Bryanston Court, Bryanston Square, W1, cancelled 21 April 1936, and bearing the inscription in red crayon, 'I think you have written a very nice article — ER', is hardly a significant piece of history, but it commands a price of £200-£300/$320-$480, equal to examples of more extensive correspondence by the same writer at an earlier age. At the great sale of the Duchess's jewels in Geneva in 1987, the world was given ample evidence of the financial cachet of objects connected with the abdication. Perhaps there was no clearer example of this than the staggering £181,000/$289,600 paid for a gold and gem-set cigarette case by Cartier of London. The front of the case is decorated with a map of Europe showing the routes and the locations of holidays taken by Edward and his guests, including Mrs Simpson, in 1934-36. This romantic souvenir in gold, enamel and gems taught the bidders a lesson in the price of love, selling at about 70 times the auctioneer's estimate.

The Royal ephemera includes written memorabilia, photographs, paintings by members of the royal families, programmes of state events, including coronations and jubilee celebrations, first-day covers and stamps, greetings cards, cigarette cards, books, tins, flags, banners and bunting, and many other catagories of collectables. Sometimes, even furniture appears in a sale of royal ephemera. Examples are an oak chair covered in blue velvet with the royal monogram, made for use in Westminster Abbey for the coronation of Queen Elizabeth II in 1953 and a red-lacquered chair with the Prince of Wales feathers in gold on the back, made for the investiture at Caernarvon Castle in 1969.

Chairs like these are not expensive collectors' items — they were barely reaching £100/$160 in the late 1980s. In fact, substantial objects like these fail to reach one-third of the value of something personally associated with royalty, such as a pair of Buckingham Palace ration books. 'Lot 245. 1949-1950 General ration book issued to HM Queen Elizabeth, and 1948-1949 Junior ration book issued to HRH Princess Margaret, *used*.' The last word, italicized by the cataloguer, was sufficient to underwrite a value of £350/$560 for these royal souvenirs of austerity days, their coupons duly ticked with the pencil cancellations of butcher and grocer 'by appointment'.

A royal connection will further enhance the value of objects which already appeal as collectors' items. In 1981, an attractive collection of 18th-, 19th- and 20th-century decorative fans came to Phillips from Kensington Palace. The 26 beautifully made and painted fans belonged to the late Princess Alice, Countess of Athlone, who had acquired them at various times in her life. Many were accompanied by labels showing that they were gifts from European royalty whose names read like a roll-call from the *Almanac de Gotha*. There was a 19th-century, black Chantilly lace fan, a present to Princess Alice from her mother, Princess Fredericka, Duchess of Albany. A similar fan came from her mother-in-law, Mary Adelaide, Duchess of Teck. From the Queen of Spain, there was a Flemish fan of about 1890, and an Edwardian example was the gift of Emma, Queen Mother of the Netherlands.

Such exalted provenance is important, but many collectables have never been anywhere near a royal household. Like commemorative china, they are mass-produced for a popular market at times of celebration. Among a range of tins (for biscuits, tea, sweets, chocolate, drawing instruments, pencils and paints) produced for Queen Elizabeth's 1977 Jubilee, one stands out — a circular tin which receives full marks for effort. An inscription emphasizes the royal connection of Kenya tea, in that the young Queen started her reign while she was staying at Tree Tops lodge, on Mount Kenya; it was there that she received the sad news of the death of her father, George VI.

Some jubilee souvenirs are rare today because they were made specifically for disposal. The Queen's Silver Jubilee appeal emblem appeared on disposable paper and plastic tableware designed for street parties — plates, cups, tablecovers and napkins. A set in pristine condition would earn its place in a collection of royal ephemera, a true 'pop' souvenir of that glorious summer's day of national jollification. A companion item might be a copy of the sheet music for the 'Silver Jubilee Souvenir Song', bearing a portrait of the Queen and the

tuneful homage, 'Ring out the bells of Jubilee for a gracious lady...' There was plenty of liquid cheer, special brews for royal occasions being a long-standing British tradition, bottles of jubilee ale from Courage displayed the official emblem and Moet & Chandon champagne, 'Silver Jubilee Cuvée, was a mere £10.95/$17.52 per magnum, £5.30/$8.48 a bottle.

The bunting of 1977 is stored away somewhere — an 11-metre (36 foot) tape bearing alternate flags and pennants, sold as a pack at £2.70/$4.32. Does anyone still wear a pair of knee socks with vertical red and white stripes and a Union Jack motif, or the jubilee bra and brief set (choose between an all-over Union Jack design and a discreet appearance of the jubilee emblem)? For 95p/$1.52 you could have joined the order of the jubilee garter by purchasing a saucy circlet of elastic trimmed with red, white and blue lace ('One size only').

Far left Silver-framed photographs of 1905, showing the future King George V and his Queen Mary; the photographs have been signed by the royal couple and inscribed 'India'. In 1987 they sold at Phillips Cardiff for more than £6,000/$9,600.

Below Souvenirs of the 1937 coronation of King George VI and Queen Elizabeth, later the Queen Mother.

The spice of life for six monarchs — that is the proud boast of Keen's, the mustard-makers, in an *Illustrated London News* special number devoted to the coronation of Edward VII in 1902.

One type of clothing never fails to attract keen bidding whenever it appears on the market — Queen Victoria's underwear. However, it is not very scarce, popping up at auction from time to time, usually in sales of textiles, priced at barely £100/$160 an item. Voluminous whitework bloomers, chemises with Valenciennes trim, ivory silk stockings and nightdresses — all formerly in the royal wardrobe — are known to the auction houses. Each piece bears the royal cipher and many are worked with a delicately embroided number similar to the cipher. It is claimed without substantiation, that the Queen usually wore her numbered pieces of underwear only once per item. There are certainly surprisingly large quantities of her royal lingerie in existence, and it is known that she was in the habit of making presents of her underwear to serving ladies and maids. Oddly enough, and whether or not she would have been amused by the phenomenon, royal underwear as a collectors' item appears to be Queen Victoria's monopoly.

Chapter 9

Play Time

Compared with the buyer of modern commemoratives, who has to pick his way through a minefield of junk, the collector of bygones is at an advantage. History helps the process of selection. The shoddy tends to disintegrate and to be discarded with the passage of time, whereas the better quality items survive. Even many of those in dubious taste became 'quaint' with age. This is true of toys with a royal theme.

In the golden years of Queen Elizabeth II's childhood, an industry in Germany and France, as well as Britain, was geared to producing curly-headed Princess Elizabeth dolls. These were often paired with the royal younger sister (those old enough will remember that she was always referred to as Princess Margaret Rose in those days). At times, — in Britain at least, it must have seemed a straight race between the royal sisters and that other curly-haired moppet' 'queen' Shirley Temple of Hollywood, as to which was the most popular doll.

A carved wooden and plaster royal event, probably made in Germany in the 1920s or 30s for a shop window display; the figures of the king and queen are about six inches in height.

Good, mediocre and downright bad, much of this large nursery of sleeping, crying (and, dare it be suggested, wetting?) dolls has long since disappeared. Poor quality often meant poor durability, and even the hardier products of the doll factories suffered heavy wear and tear. A bisque-headed Princess Elizabeth doll of the late 1920s or early 1930s, marked *'Porzellanfabrik Burggrub'*, and in good condition can be worth a few thousand pounds. In fact a well-worn survivor attracted keen bidding, even though she was gownless and hairless.

A fairly rare British version of the Princess Elizabeth doll was produced by Chad Valley in 1930. It was a 43-cm (17-in) portrait doll 'Approved by Her Royal Highness the Duchess of York'. A chubby princess with short, curly blonde hair wore a pearl necklace and a dress with tiers of frills. Princess Elizabeth dolls dating from the end of the 1930s are rather commoner than this 1930 example. Chad Valley produced the royal sisters in velveteen, fully jointed.

Hair was hand woven and the dresses, modelled on the real Princess' contemporary fashions, were pink or blue. Princess Elizabeth was obtainable in 46- or 53-cm (18- or 21-in) sizes; she wore a hat and a double-breasted coat over a flowered dress or a party frock. Princess Margaret, 41-cm (16-in) tall, was similarly dressed. The dolls, just as much as newsreel and press pictures of the Princesses, influenced the fashions of countless middle-class children in Britain and in particular popularized the double-breasted coat.

The value of royal dolls has been steadily increasing in recent years and is expected to continue to do so. This has little to do with topical royal events such as a much publicized wedding or jubilee, but has its roots in the general rise of doll collecting. American interest, as always, is a great spur to the market.

Among tomorrow's antiques are several dolls and similar items produced at the time of Queen Elizabeth II's Silver Jubilee in

1977, some of which were displayed at the Commemorative Collectors' Society exhibition at the Goldsmiths Hall in London. An outstanding example was the Queen doll, made in a limited edition of 500 by a specialist manufacturer, Peggy Nisbet, of Weston-Super-Mare in the west of England. The model wears evening dress, tiara, necklace, Garter sash and star and family orders on the shoulder, and is seated in a gilded and upholstered chair. The head, arms and legs of the doll are in white bone china and it has a white leather body. At the expensive issue price of more than £36/$57.60, it was destined to be a display piece, rather than a toy. Collectors would now expect to pay a considerable premium for the doll.

The same maker also produced another 500 edition doll. Costing £11, it was exclusive to Hamley's, the famous London toy store, and was much more of a plaything. Again from Nisbet, who was heavily represented in the

society's choice, came three 'fun' toys: a cuddly lion sporting a scarlet crown, a nutmeg-coloured teddy bear wearing a satin tunic with the jubilee motif, and an 'unbreakable' royal herald in court dress. Children of an earlier age, it seems, had no such frivolity offered to them: dolls of Queen Victoria are solemn-looking and wear voluminous gowns and brocaded and beaded decoration. Nevertheless, their somewhat forbidding appearance is no bar to prices of more than £1,000/$1,600 when a modest example in good condition comes to auction.

It is worth noting that a flood of contemporary royal commemoratives can depress the market for older items. A sale of lead soldiers at Phillips in 1981 included more than 200 figures, by Timpo, of the Queen mounted on her famous horse Winston. These models, dating from the 1950s, came from the stock of an old toy shop. They would nornally have been expected to fetch about £5-£8/$8-$12.80 each

(multiply by three to allow for inflation). The dealer who bought the majority at an average £2/$3.20 each shrugged his shoulders when he was asked if he expected to make a 'killing' in the year of Prince Charles's wedding, with all its attendant royal 'mania'. 'No,' he said, 'there are too many tourist souvenirs about. I'll just put them in stock and bide my time.'

Manufacturers of lead soldiers, especially the firm of William Britain, the pioneer of the hollow-cast figure, have been a good, consistent source of 'royal' toys and models. Paradoxically, in the royal wedding year of 1981, the auction price for a Britain's coronation coach or the royal state landau bearing the Queen and Prince Philip was less than it had been a couple of years earlier. The reason was simple that good prices realized at auction had brought a procession of these coaches out of attics and store cupboards and so the auction price had fallen. It has since recovered and they are healthily

Left Advertisements such as this one in 1902 for Lemco's meat extract show that somewhat cavalier attitudes prevailed towards the use of the crown and royalty in commercial claims. Some enthusiasts make a point of collecting 'royal' ads.

Right Royalty in the pocket. A silver vesta, or match, case bearing the portrait of Edward VII and hallmarked in Birmingham 1901; 2in (5cm) in length, worth **£100-plus/$160-plus**.

A delightful little mug made for Harrods at the time of Queen Victoria's diamond jubilee in 1897. It is printed in brown and decorated in coloured enamels, with a portrait and sporting scenes; £50-£100/$80-$160.

in demand now when they appear for sale.

Coronation coaches have had a chequered career in the collectors' market. In the early 1970s, the formative years of the toy soldier boom, a post-war Lesney coach, which is smaller scale than Britain's reached the then remarkable figure of £60/$96. It was, as the auctioneers were first to admit, something of a fluke. When Lesney coaches flooded the salerooms and glutted the market, the price dropped to its real level of a few pounds. Eventually, the auctioneers refused to put them into sales unless other items accompanied them 'to make up a lot.'

Other royal models from Britian's included some historical characters, such as Henry VIII and his six wives, various kings and queens in ceremonial robes or mounted on horseback, and an attractive gilt model of the coronation chair. John Hill and Company (Johillco), the nearest

British rival to Britain's in the pre- and post-war periods, scored a success among their young customers with a small-scale coronation procession of King George VI, complete with Horse and Life Guards, footmen and Yeomen of the Guard.

Juvenilia with a royal flavour includes jigsaw puzzles, games, picture books, playing cards, lantern slides and similar bric-a-brac. Each has its own following and each has steadily appreciated in price over the past decade, values depending on the quality and rarity of individual items.

Perhaps the royal 'toy' to beat all others was the panther onyx and diamond bracelet which the Duke of Windsor gave to his Duchess in 1952. It is a slinky, articulated feline with emerald eyes, made by Cartier of Paris. It was sold for £860,000/$1,376,000 in the 1987 auction of the Windsor jewels.

Chapter 10

Advice for Collectors

Large quantities of commemorative china have been ruined and drastically reduced in value by the use of harsh washing soda over the years. Like the dustbin syndrome, this emphasizes the value of those items which have survived in good condition — and condition is a prime factor in the choosing of commemoratives, as it is in practically every field of collecting.

Any specialist dealer or auction house cataloguer will give the same advice to a beginner: buy the best your pocket can afford and buy only those pieces in good, preferably pristine, condition. Sometimes a chip or a crack may be acceptable if the rarity of an item outweighs all other considerations. But, on the whole, mint condition is important, not only to the owner's enjoyment of a

Signed photographs, letters, a fan, cards and programmes make up a small haul from a typical auction of royal ephemera.

collection, but it will count critically if he or she wishes to dispose of possessions or 'trade up' in quality. (Enhancing a collection in this way, as taste becomes more sophisticated or specialized, is one of the joys of collecting.) With modern techniques of restoration, a damaged plate or a mug can be convincingly treated, but always remember that repairs are expensive and the cost may turn a 'bargain' into a minor financial liability.

The beginner must study the subject thoroughly. Many museums throughout the country have displays of commemorative china, but the best way to become acquainted with it is at auction views. These are usually held on one or two days before the sale, and the viewer is able to handle the pieces — a privilege obviously denied to the museum visitor. The occasion presents a unique opportunity of close acquaintance with objects of widely different type and quality. Similarly, monitoring the progress of a few auctions will give the would-be collector an overall view of demand and values. If you are planning to bid at auction, read the catalogue carefully so that you know what you are buying. Some lots comprise a number of pieces. It may be that you will have your sights on, say, half a dozen items scattered through different lots. It is not unknown for collectors to extract their chosen pieces from, say, three or four lots for which they have successfully bid, then consign the remaining unwanted pieces to an auction at a later date to recover some of their costs.

Apart from sales at the major auction houses (of both commemorative china and royal ephemera), there are now many specialist dealers, too numerous to list. Royal souvenir china is also to be found in countless general antique shops and markets. It crops up in quantity at antique fairs and swap meets. Book barrows and shops dealing in old prints, postcards and the like often yield royal ephemera such as coronation programmes, old picture books and magazines — even the odd signed photograph of royalty.

A 'must' for every collector of royalty is membership of the Commemorative Collectors' Society. Full details of the annual subscription (a bargain) and the service the organization provides may be obtained from Steven N. Jackson, Secretary, Commemorative Collectors' Society, 25 Farndale Close, Long Eaton, near Nottingham, NG10 3PA. The society was founded in 1972 by a group of commemorative collectors 'as a non-commercial and non-profit-making body, to represent the interests of a growing number of collectors throughout the world, to stimulate a wider interest and understanding of "popular" commemorative pieces in all media by providing information and promoting research into the historical and social background which promoted the issue of such items'. A regular quarterly journal, packed with information and illustrations, goes to some 4,500 members in 32 countries. Meetings are organized by the society at museums and similar venues, at which guest speakers give talks on specialized commemorative subjects. The society also assists, sponsors or organizes exhibitions. Since its inception, it has mounted five major exhibitions — each a milestone in commemorative lore — the catalogues of which are now jealously guarded collectors' treasures.

Steven Jackson estimates that more than 82 per cent of the society's members collect memorabilia covering the British and other royal families; items are regularly issued in the Netherlands, Denmark, Norway, Sweden, Belgium and Monaco, with Spain fast catching up. He takes pains to emphasize that the subject of ephemera has a significant place in the affections of commemorative collectors. 'Our interest coverage includes ceramics, glass, printed tins, printed and woven fabrics, enamels, jigsaw puzzles, postcards, gramaphone records, prints and printed ephemera such as souvenir editions of *The Illustrated London News, The Graphic, Sphere, Everybody's* and *Picture Post* as well as *Radio Times* and *TV Times,* books of all kinds and special souvenir programmes.'

Interest is not limited to royalty, although that topic is uppermost. Chosen at random, an edition of the society's journal for autumn 1985 illustrates, among many other items, the following eclectic bag of commemoratives: a portrait plate of King Albert of the Belgians, another for the Abraham Lincoln centenary of 1909, tankards celebrating Edwardian actresses, a satin pennant for King Juan Carlos of Spain, a mug to mark a visit to Colchester by Queen Elizabeth, a VE-day thimble with a portrait of Winston Churchill, a mug commemorating the Conservative victory in Britain's 1983 general election, a porcelain candle-holder depicting Margaret Thatcher and Arthur Scargill, the leader of the National Union of Mineworkers, eyeball to eyeball, and President Reagan as a coffee pot with turned

up nose/spout.

Searching for the unusual and the rare is part of the fun in collecting. Britannia, Rita and Ian Smythe's shop at Gray's Antique Market, in the West End of London, is a happy and glorious sight to behold, with thousands of pieces of china royalty on parade. 'The great joy about collecting is the chance of the unknown turning up,' said Ian Smythe. 'We've sold tens of thousands of pieces over the last two decades, but every two months or so we come across an item we never knew existed.' The Smythes admit to a 'small, very eccentric' private collection of royal commemoratives which are 'oddities with unflattering likenesses, and that sort of thing'. You could call it a collection of ugly mugs.

A collector may start by buying a variety of pieces, representing several reigns. Eventually, however, most enthusiasts begin to specialize and this is to be recommended. The choice is immense. The products of Queen Victoria's reign are an obvious option, but the field is so wide that the collector may wish to concentrate on jubilee items, on Prince Albert, the royal children, or simply on Victorian plates or jugs. Another area of specialization would be beakers, mugs and plates bearing inscriptions relating to municipalities — the mayors' handouts to schoolchildren and the poor. Single-factory source as a specialization defines a field, yet offers scope over many reigns. The life of Edward VIII is popular; some people collect only items relating to the abdication while others concentrate on ephemera related to the years when the Duke and Duchess of Windsor lived abroad. In the realm of ephemera, royal autograph letters, photographs, official coronation programmes, greetings cards and state invitations are just a few of the specialized subjects available. Sooner or later, the enthusiast comes to the truth that specialization is the heart and soul of collecting. Long may it reign.

Right Ten military aspects of King Edward VII, including honorary colonelcies of Prussian, Hungarian and Russian regiments: a series of cigarette cards issued by Edwards, Ringer and Bigg, and worth £150-£200/$240-$320 per set.

Below A magnificent souvenir of Victorian postal history. 'The Queen's Own' of 1842 was a printed pictorial envelope for use by patriotic correspondents. This one was used in Edinburgh; nearly a century and a half later, it sold at auction for £6,600/$10,560.

Below King William III (1689-1702) appears in crowned splendour on an English Delft plate of Brislington, near Bath. It is a rare piece, price at nearly £5,000 in 1984.

Books listed by the Commemorative Collectors' Society:
COMMEMORATIVE POTTERY 1780-1900, John and Jenifer May, Heinemann, London.
COMMEMORATIVE POTTERY AND PORCELAIN, James Mackay, Garnstone Press, London.
CORONATION SOUVENIRS, David Rodgers, Latimers New Dimension.

Acknowledgements

The author's thanks go to the staff of Phillips; in particular, to Andrew Hilton and his specialists in the Collectors' Centre; to Christopher Halton, Diana Kay and Jacqueline Barber for their help in providing illustrations, of which the great majority come from Phillips; and to Paul Penn-Simkins. Gratitude is owed to Rita and Ian Smythe, of Britannia in London, whose knowledge and experience of royal commemoratives has been generously shared, both in the written and the spoken word, over the years. A considerable contribution to this book has been made by the Commemorative Collectors Society: its various publications have been a source of inspiration and information; and, especially, the author thanks its secretary, Steven N. Jackson, for his enthusiasm and assistance.